Quotable Cats

summersdale

QUOTABLE CATS

Summersdale Publishers Ltd
46 West Street
Chichester
West Sussex
PO19 1RP
UK

www.summersdale.com

Printed and bound by Tien Wah Press, Singapore

All images © Shutterstock

ISBN: 1-84024-536-0
ISBN: 978-1-84024-536-3

Quotable Cats

There are **no ordinary** cats.

Colette

To **bathe a cat** takes brute force, perseverance, courage of conviction – and a cat. The **last ingredient** is usually hardest to come by.

Stephen Baker

A cat's got her own opinion of human beings. She don't **say much**, but you can tell **enough** to make you anxious not to hear the whole of it.

Jerome K. Jerome

Cats are the **ultimate narcissists.**
You can tell this because of all the **time** they
spend on personal grooming.

James Gorman

The **smallest** feline is a masterpiece.

Leonardo da Vinci

They say the **test** of literary power is whether a man can write an inscription. I say 'Can he **name a kitten**?'

Samuel Butler

Cats are a **mysterious** kind of folk. There is more passing in their **minds** than we are aware of.

Sir Walter Scott

If it's **raining** at the back door, every cat is convinced there's a **good chance** that it won't be raining at the front door.

For me, one of the pleasures of cats' **company** is their devotion to bodily comfort.

Sir Compton Mackenzie

Cats are intended to teach us that **not everything** in nature has a **purpose**.

Garrison Keillor

Happiness does not light gently on my shoulder like a butterfly. She pounces on my lap, demanding that I scratch behind her ears.

Anonymous

Cats are **smarter than dogs.** You can't get eight cats to pull a sled through snow.

Jeff Valdez

Women and cats will do as they please, and men and dogs should **relax** and get used to the idea.

Robert A. Heinlein

The **last thing** I would accuse a cat of is **innocence**.

Edward Paley

What **greater gift** than the **love** of a cat?

Charles Dickens

Thousands of years ago, cats were **worshipped as gods.** Cats have never forgotten this.

Anonymous

There is **no snooze** button on a cat who wants breakfast.

Anonymous

Even **overweight cats** instinctively know the cardinal rule: when fat, arrange yourself in **slim poses**.

John Weitz

The cat does **not offer services**. The cat offers itself.

William S. Burroughs

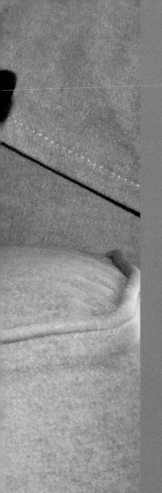

If you want to be a psychological **novelist** and write about human beings, the best thing you can do is own a **pair of cats**.

Aldous Huxley

Way **down deep** we are all
motivated by the **same urges.**
Cats have the **courage** to live
by them.

Jim Davies

The **trouble with** cats is that they've got no tact.

P. G. Wodehouse

There is something about the **presence** of a cat... that seems to take **the bite** out of being alone.

Louis Camuti

When a cat **adopts** you, there is nothing to be done about it except to **put up with** it and wait until the wind changes.

T. S. Eliot

It was soon noticed that when there was **work** to be done the cat could **never** be found.

George Orwell

People that hate **cats** will come back as **mice** in their next life.

Faith Resnick

Cats **do not** have to be shown how to have a **good** time, for they are unfailing **ingenious** in that respect.

James Mason

No matter how much **cats fight**, there always seems to be **plenty** of kittens.

Abraham Lincoln

Cats have **enormous** patience with the limitations of the human mind.

Cleveland Amory

Dogs have owners, **cats** have **staff.**

Rita Mae Brown

The way to get on with a cat is to treat it as **an equal** – or even better, as the **superior** it knows itself to be.

Elizabeth Peters

I should not feel quite easy in the **company** of any cat that walked about the house with a **saintly** expression.

Beverly Nichols

A cat can **purr** its way out of anything.

Donna McCrohan

A cat is there when you **call** her – if she doesn't have something **better** to do.

Bill Adler

Cats always seem so **very wise**, when staring with their **half-closed** eyes.

Bette Midler

The **problem** with cats is that they get the exact **same look** on their face whether they see a **moth** or an axe-murderer.

Paula Poundstone

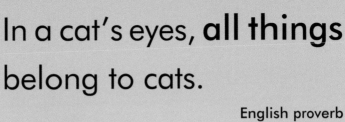

In a cat's eyes, **all things** belong to cats.

English proverb

I've met many thinkers and many cats, but the **wisdom of cats** is infinitely **superior.**

Hippolyte Taine

It is a very **inconvenient habit** of kittens that whatever **you say** to them, they always purr.

Lewis Carroll

To err is human,

to **purr** feline.

Robert Byrne

The cat. He walked **by himself**, and **all** places were alike to him.

Rudyard Kipling

If man could be crossed with the cat it would **improve** the man, but it would **deteriorate the cat.**

Mark Twain

When my cats aren't happy, I'm not **happy**. Not because I care about their **mood** but because I know they're just sitting there **thinking** up ways to get even.

Percy Bysshe Shelley

Cats are **only human**, they have their faults.

Kingsley Amis

Time spent with cats is never wasted.

Sigmund Freud

Quotable Dogs

Quotable Dogs

£5.99

ISBN: 1-84024-537-9
ISBN: 978-1-84024-537-0

No matter how little money and how few possessions you own, having a dog makes you rich.

Louis Sabin

A stunning photographic book with quotes about canines, this delightful celebration of your best friend and loyal companion is a pooch of a gift for every dog-lover.

www.summersdale.com